Avoid living in a Wild West Town

Written by
Peter Hicks

Illustrated by
David Antram

Created and designed by
David Salariya

The Danger Zone

BOOK HOUSE

Contents

Introduction   5

Welcome to Dustville!   6

Look out – stampede!   8

The cowboys are in town!   10

The buffalo hunt   12

Law and order   14

Boot Hill   16

Sickness and disease   18

Indians!   20

Braving the weather   22

Fun and entertainment   24

Later at night...   26

You meet your end!   28

Glossary   30

Index   32

Introduction

fter the American Civil War (1861-1865) ended, the Great Plains were opened up. Cowboys herded millions of cattle across these vast expanses of grassland west of the Mississippi river. Farmers tried to grow crops on the plains and hunters killed the buffalo that grazed on them. This was a dangerous place to be. The Plains Indians – Sioux, Crow, Pawnee, Cheyenne, Comanche and Kiowa – fought hard to protect their land. People living there suffered in the heat of the summer and froze in the winter. Soon settlements sprung up. To start with, these were just a few ex-army tents selling basic supplies. If they were in a good spot they became towns, providing goods and services for the men trying to make a living there. Life in these towns was often uncomfortable, dangerous and violent. They attracted all sorts – the good, the bad and the wild. Your name is Jim McGuire and you are the marshal of one such town called Dustville. You are more than qualified to understand why you wouldn't want to live in a wild west town!

Welcome to Dustville!

Early one morning, you take a stroll down Main Street, Dustville, the place you call home. Main Street is the busiest part of town. There is a whole range of businesses here, from shops and hotels to theatres and bars. The shopkeepers can supply you with your every need – clothing, boots, groceries, beef-steaks, saddles, pistols, rifles, ammunition and even haircuts! Everything for the farmer, cowboy, buffalo hunter, traveller, cattleman or townsman can be found here. Remember to tip your hat politely to the town mayor when you pass him – he is your employer after all!

As usual, you try hard to ignore the dust everywhere. During dry spells nothing stops it from flying. Horses, wagons and the stagecoach make it worse, and it lands on everybody and everything.

Handy hint

Avoid making eye contact with strangers. They might think you're looking for a fight!

Morning, Mayor!

Look out – stampede!

Turning a corner, you walk straight into a trail herd that has just arrived in town! It's a herd of longhorn cattle that cowboys have driven up from Texas. They're noisy, dangerous and smelly – and that's just the cowboys! In Texas longhorns are worth $4 each, but in the northern cities they sell for $40 and this trade makes Dustville prosperous. Longhorns are unpopular with local farmers because of the 'Texas fever'. This contagious disease is carried by longhorns and it could wipe out the local cattle. The longhorns are therefore kept away from local farms.

Jingle

THE LONGHORN is a tough breed. They can be any colour and weigh between 350 and 450 kg. The horns can reach two metres from end to end!

250,000 longhorns pass through the cattle pens in Dustville every year. It's a very big business.

TRAINS carry the cattle from Dustville to Chicago, their final destination.

Yikes!

YELP!

CRAAACK!

Handy hint

Make sure your home is nowhere near the noisy cattle pens, or you'll never get any sleep!

The cowboys are in town!

What they wear:

A WIDE-BRIM HAT as protection against the sun, rain and snow.

A KNOTTED HANDKERCHIEF for use as a breathing mask, bandage and water filter.

A LEATHER VEST for keeping safe a watch, tobacco and money.

A HOLSTER AND GUN BELT although not all cowboys wear these. Guns and ammunition are expensive.

LEATHER BOOTS which are good for protection but difficult to walk in.

No sooner have the cattle noisily passed by than the cowboys who have just herded them up start to cause trouble. These men have been in the saddle for two months and they've just been paid. You are called in to stop an argument over money and you nearly get your head knocked off in the process! These men deserve their pay of $60 for the hard work, danger and boredom of the last eight weeks. They have faced wind and rain, and have rescued their cattle from quicksand, mud and barbed wire. They have been shot at by unfriendly farmers and lived on a diet of beans, bacon and biscuits! All they want now is a bath, a shave, a haircut, clean clothes and a good meal. Then they will go out and enjoy themselves, although some might get a little bit out of control...

LEATHER CHAPS to protect their legs from bushes, thorns and cattle horns.

SPURS to speed up their horses.

The buffalo hunt

You stop to greet two blood-soaked friends who have just returned to town with a bulging wagon full of buffalo skins. The nearby plains are teeming with buffalo and good money is to be made from killing them. Their skins are sold for $3 each and made into leather.

However, the trade is not without its risks. Buffalo are very nervous animals and stampedes are common. Since the hunters are killing the main food supply of the Plains Indians, they are also often attacked.

The buffalo hunt

SHOOTING. Buffalo hunters use a heavy .50 calibre rifle with a range of 550 metres.

SKINNING. Captured buffalo are skinned where they fall. Teams use mules to help in this gruesome process.

Yes, a good day's kill today!

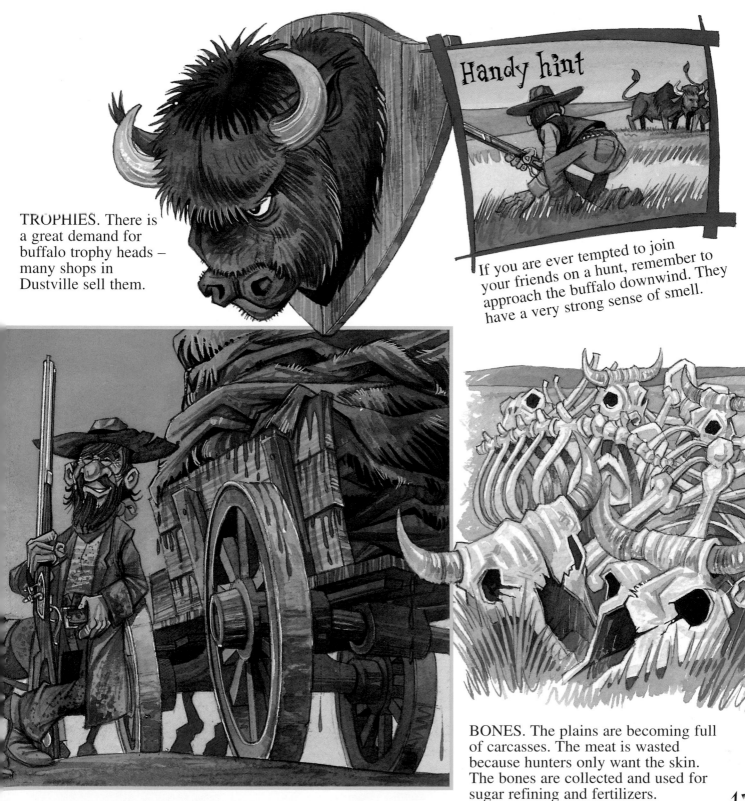

TROPHIES. There is a great demand for buffalo trophy heads – many shops in Dustville sell them.

Handy hint

If you are ever tempted to join your friends on a hunt, remember to approach the buffalo downwind. They have a very strong sense of smell.

BONES. The plains are becoming full of carcasses. The meat is wasted because hunters only want the skin. The bones are collected and used for sugar refining and fertilizers.

Law and order

Weapons

Many shops in town sell the latest pistols and rifles. However, they're not cheap.

Dustville has a reputation for being a rough and violent town and it is your job to uphold law and order. It's always worse when the cowboys are in town. Fights often break out over money. Sometimes gunfights involve innocent bystanders, who also have to dodge the bullets!

Run for your life!

LYNCHING. It has been known for hated criminals to be broken out of jail by a mob taking the law into their own hands. The criminal is strung up from the nearest tree.

Handy hint

If you're caught in a gunfight, hit the ground quick!

Oh no – my new shirt's ruined!

Boot Hill

Gunfights are unfortunately becoming increasingly common. So many people are dying in gunfights that a new place has to be found to bury them all. You decide to use a rocky, craggy hill just west of town. Nothing much grows on it and it drains well because it is a hill. A local shopkeeper doubles up as the undertaker when someone is killed.

He builds a quick pine coffin, puts it on his hearse and takes it to the waiting grave, freshly dug by the gravedigger. If the dead person is a famous outlaw, he has his picture taken with the open coffin!

Sickness and disease

You might get:

SCURVY. This is a common disease resulting from a poor diet and lack of vitamin C. It makes your gums bleed and your teeth fall out.

TUBERCULOSIS is an infectious disease of the lungs. The symptom is a continual cough that often brings up blood.

Shiver

stinky skunk

CHOLERA is a lethal disease, usually spread by infected water.

You have a terrible toothache, but there is no proper dentist, so reluctantly you decide to visit the blacksmith instead. You soon wish you hadn't! Health is a problem in Dustville. It is not a clean place and the death rate from disease, especially for children, is high. There are no sewers, so you make do with cesspits, which overflow when it rains. Flies are a constant problem because of the vast amount of manure dropped by the longhorns. In these conditions infections spread easily. Also, the first doctors in Dustville are not well-trained – they make mistakes and many people die.

Take it away!

RABIES is a very serious disease, spread by skunks who bite people while they sleep. Most people die from it, and survivors are often brain damaged. Sufferers have a dread of water.

Indians!

Dustville today is particularly tense, as a party of Cheyenne Indians has come into town to make some complaints. Sitting down with them and listening carefully, you can understand why they are angry. A recent treaty allows the local Cheyenne, Comanche and Kiowa tribes the sole hunting rights north of their territory up as far as the Dust River. However, white hunters tempted by the high prices of buffalo skins have been crossing the river onto their land.

Hmmm – I see...

TEPEES. The plains tribes are hunter-gatherers, so they are often on the move. Tepees allow them to set up and take down their villages quickly.

Handy hint

If you're tempted to go into Indian Territory looking for rich pickings, don't go alone. You may be picked off in an ambush and never seen again.

INDIAN ATTACK! Angered by the destruction of their buffalo herds, Indians sometimes attack lonely farms.

WEAPONS. Steel has made traditional weapons like the tomahawk and spear even sharper. Bows and arrows are deadly and the war club, a polished pointed stone, has a long reach.

21

Braving the weather

Dustville is very exposed to all kinds of weather. When it rains, Main Street is turned into a river of slimy mud, up to half a metre deep. Shopkeepers provide long wooden platforms in front of their shops, and planks are laid across the street for pedestrians, but the mud gets everywhere. During the winter, blizzards pile up massive snow drifts, cutting off Dustville for weeks on end and making food supplies run short.

DUST STORMS are a hazard in the summer. You can't see a thing and the dust gets into your lungs.

FIRE is another danger. Fires are sometimes caused by lightning strikes, but more often by someone being careless with a candle.

LAST WINTER was particularly cold. Thousands of cattle were frozen to death in blizzards.

HEAVE!

Handy hint

If you get caught out on the plains in a blizzard, kill a buffalo and take out its intestines. Climb in and its body warmth will keep you alive!

23

Fun and entertainment

Your choice:

PRIZE FIGHTS are popular in town and seen as a great opportunity for betting.

Thwack!

THE RODEO, a chance for cowboys to show off their skills, is watched by hundreds.

HORSE RACES also take place regularly. Fast starters and sprinters fetch very high prices.

As evening approaches, you have revellers and party-goers to deal with. For many cowboys, who have been working hard for months, Dustville seems like paradise, full of comfort, fun and entertainment.

24

There are many theatres. The most popular one is in Main Street. Plays, concerts and comedy shows all do the rounds regularly, with mixed success. Some cowboys make life very unpleasant for entertainers who aren't very good and you often have to calm things down. Other activities reflect the outdoor life. Hunting is popular both as a sport and a source of meat. Dustville greyhounds are famous for their hunting abilities.

Handy hint

Prize-fight organisers are clever. The authorities do not approve so they only tell their regular spectators the time and place. A 4.30 a.m. start is fine. You and your deputies will be fast asleep!

Later at night...

Many cowboys head for the dance halls in the later evenings. Lots of the hotels also have billiard halls, which are popular places for friends to gather. As the night progresses, things often get increasingly rowdy and your evenings are usually busy enough just trying to keep the peace. However, some dance-hall owners take the law into their own hands and police the halls themselves.

> This is going to hurt when I land!

GAMBLING is also common in Dustville. Many cowboys and hunters lose all of their hard-earned cash to professional gamblers in the bars.

BARS are the main cause of trouble in Dustville. Men gather in them to drink, talk and chew tobacco. They spit tobacco juice into containers called spittoons – disgusting!

You meet your end!

You are a popular marshal. You are friendly, carry out your duties well and never run from trouble. You are respected by the townspeople for doing a difficult job in dangerous circumstances. However, one day two cowhands hit town and start looking for you. They are abusive, threatening and fully armed. They tell anyone who will listen that you murdered their brother last year and they're 'gonna get you'. You turn the corner and walk straight into them...

IN A BLAZE OF GUNFIRE you fall to the ground. You have been hit in the stomach. The locals look on in horror.

IT LOOKS BAD. 'I've been shot', you groan, as two of your friends pick you up and carry you to the nearest doctor.

YOUR INJURIES ARE SEVERE. Although the doctor does all he can, you die 40 minutes later.

AS A SIGN OF MOURNING all the businesses in Dustville close for the day and the shop fronts are draped in black.

YOU ARE BURIED at the mayor's expense in a little plot next to the town's chapel. Of course, Boot Hill is not for you.

LIFE MUST GO ON and the mayor has to appoint your successor. After the funeral he pins the badge on the new marshal – your brother!

29

Glossary

Ambush A surprise attack from a hidden position.

American Civil War A war fought between the Southern states (Confederacy) and the Northern states (Union) of America between 1861 and 1865.

Ammunition Bullets that are fired from guns.

Blizzard A violent snow storm.

Buckskin Leather from a deer.

Calibre Width of the barrel of a gun.

Carcasses Dead bodies of animals.

Cesspits Holes dug in the ground to contain human sewage.

Chaps A piece of clothing made of leather and worn over trousers to protect a cowboy's legs.

Contagious Easily spread by close contact.

Cowhand Another word for cowboy.

Fertilizer Material that makes the soil better for growing plants in.

Hearse A vehicle used to carry dead bodies to the place of burial.

Holster A leather holder for a pistol.

Lynching The killing of a suspected criminal without a trial.

Marshal The chief peace officer of a town.

Mayor The person who is in charge of a town. He is elected by the people.

Outlaw A person on the run from the law.

Plains Indians Tribes of American Indians who lived on the Great Plains west of the Mississippi river.

Quicksand Loose, wet and deep sand that is easy to sink into.

Refining Removing impurities.

Revellers People having a good time and celebrating.

Rodeo An exhibition of cowboy skills.

Saddle horn The front of a saddle. Ropes can be tied to it.

Sewers Underground channels or pipes for carrying away sewage.

Skunk A black and white, bushy-tailed American animal.

Spur A spiked wheel fixed to the heel of a cowboy's boot. It is used to kick a horse so that it will go faster.

Stagecoach A horse-drawn coach carrying passengers to towns along a set route.

Steer A young male cow.

Tepee A tent made of soft animal hide stretched over long wooden poles.

Trail herd A large group of cattle driven long distances to a particular destination.

Undertaker A person who prepares dead bodies for burial or cremation.

Wagons Four-wheeled vehicles made of wood for carrying heavy loads.

Index

A
ambush 21, 30
American Civil War 5, 30
ammunition 6, 10, 30

B
bars 6, 26, 27
billiard halls 26
blizzard 22, 30
Boot Hill 16-17, 29
buckskin 11, 30
buffalo 5, 12, 13, 20, 21, 23
buffalo carcasses 12-13, 30

C
cattle 5, 8-9, 10, 11, 22, 31
  steers 11, 31
cemeteries 17
cesspits 18, 30
chapel 29
chaps 10, 30
cholera 18
clothing 6, 10
cowboys 5, 6, 10-11, 14, 24, 25,
  26, 30, 31
crops 5

D
dance halls 26
dentist 18
disease 18-19
doctors 18, 28
dust 7, 22

E
entertainment 24-25

F
farmers 5, 6, 8, 10
farms 8, 20
fertilizer 13, 30
fights/fighting 7, 10, 14, 24, 25
fire 22
food 10

G
gambling 26
Great Plains 5, 12, 13, 23, 31
gunfights 14-15, 16, 17
guns 10, 17, 30
  pistols 6, 14, 27, 30
  rifles 6, 12, 14

H
hearse 16, 30
holster 10, 30
horse racing 24
horses 7, 31
hotels 6, 26
hunters/hunting 5, 6, 12-13, 20,
  25, 26

I
Indians 5, 12, 20-21, 30

L
law and order 14-15
longhorns 8, 18
lynching 15, 30

M
marshal 5, 28, 29, 30
mayor 6, 29, 30
Mississippi river 5

O
outlaws 16, 30

Q
quicksand 10, 31

R
rabies 18
rodeo 24, 31

S
saddles 6, 10, 11, 31
scurvy 18
sewers 18, 31
shops 6, 22, 29

skunks 18, 31
spittoons 26
spurs 10, 31
stagecoach 7, 31

T
tepees 21, 31
Texas fever 8
theatres 6, 25
trail herds 8, 31
trains 8
tuberculosis 18

U
undertaker 16, 31

W
wagons 7, 31
weapons 20
weather 10, 12, 22-23